Patchwork & Quilting

cushions

Patchwork, Quilting & Appliqué

Patchwork & Quilting

cushions

Patchwork, Quilting & Appliqué

■ **Elaine Hammond** ■

Published by Traplet Publications Limited 1997
Traplet House,
Severn Drive,
Upton-upon-Severn,
Worcestershire. WR8 0JL
United Kingdom.

ISBN 1 900371 12 X

*Front and Back Cover
A selection of cushions.*

Technical drawings reproduced by Lee Wisedale

Book Design by Sue Huxley

Photography by Jerry Mullaney

Printed and bound by Stephens & George Limited,
Merthyr Industrial Estate, Dowlais, Merthyr Tydfil, Mid Glamorgan CF48 2TD

acknowledgments

With thanks to the great team at Traplet for all their help, to Dianne Huck for proofing and advice, and Avril Hopcraft for her help with completing all these cushions.

Thanks are also due to the Patchwork & Quilting readers, whose enthusiasm and imagination in turn ignite mine – I never lack for ideas, especially when I have spent time with my fellow quilters.

I hope you will find this an enjoyable and inspiring book – I would love to see your interpretations of these designs.

contents

introduction

Cushions are useful everywhere, but they need not be plain and boring! Brighten up your surroundings with some of the ideas in this book, and learn patchwork techniques at the same time. Plan the colours to accent and lighten a dark room perhaps, and even the car can benefit from some cheering up and comfort!

Cushions have been around for ever, I expect even cavemen made themselves comfortable on bundles of fur. I was interested to read the other day that Bess of Hardwick (Elizabeth, Countess of Shrewsbury) who spent fortunes rebuilding and decorating her family home, Hardwick Hall in 1590, listed 'too long quitions (cushions) of Cloth of golde and red damask, one of them lyned with russet velvet, the other with washcolored satin bridges(?)' amongst her new acquisitions. They sound, as Thomas Lake said, 'like comfortable pieces of art.'

I also looked up the word cushion in Brewer's Dictionary of Phrase and Fable and discovered the following:

Cushion Dance: A lively dance, popular in early Stuart times, in which kissing while kneeling on a cushion was a major feature. It survived quite late in rural districts. John Clare (1793-1864), the peasant poet of Northamptonshire, mentions it in his May-Day Ballad:

And then comes the cushion, the girls they all shriek,

And fly to the door from the fiddler's squeak:

But the doors they are fastened, so all must kneel down,

And take the rude kiss from th'unmannerly clown.

Sounds like fun doesn't it?

I hope you will find inspiration for some interesting cushions in this book – do let us see them at Traplet Publications – and that you will enjoy the pleasure of making your own comfortable pieces of art.

To make the best use of this book it is worth noting the following:

- All cushions are graded with this symbol

  1 for easy, 2 for moderate and 3 for difficult. All can be managed if you take your time and read the instructions carefully, but if you are a beginner you should be aware that the higher graded projects will be more difficult and time consuming.

- It is assumed throughout this book that the fabric width you are using is 45" (112cm).

- A soft, well worn old cotton sheet makes an excellent backing for quilting.

- It is assumed that the usual sewing kit – thimble, scissors for paper and fabric, needles and pins etc. as well as pens and pencils, card etc will be available.

- Both metric and imperial measurements are given – use one or the other but don't mix them.

curved heart *cushions*

This cushion is sweetly romantic and would be ideal for a teenagers bedroom. Although the seams are curved, they won't be too difficult if you take your time. The quilting is drawn on free hand – the design is hugs and kisses as used by youngsters on birthday cards and letters.

REQUIREMENTS

Finished Size: 16" (41cm) square

- 1 yard (1 metre) plain pink fabric
- ¼ yard (.25m) patterned pink fabric
- ¼ yard (.25m) white or cream fabric
- 18" (46cm) square of 2oz. wadding
- 18" (46cm) square of spare fabric for back of quilting
- 1 x 16" (41cm) cushion pad
- Matching thread for sewing
- Pink quilting thread

TO MAKE: curved heart *cushions*

1. Cut 2 pieces 17" x 4" (44cm x 10cm) and two pieces 2½" x 9½" (6.5cm x 24cm) plain pink fabric. Lay the rest aside for the cushion back.

2. Cut 6 Template B in pink flowered fabric, 2 Template B in white fabric.

3. Cut 2 Template A in pink floral fabric and 6 Template A in white fabric.

4. Cut 2 Template C in white fabric, and 2 Template C in floral fabric.

5. Join together the A and B pieces where appropriate, clipping the curve as you go to make the sewing easier. Fig. 1.

6. Lay the pieced blocks out together with the solid blocks as shown in Fig. 2.

7. Sew all the blocks together.

8. Add the two pieces 2½" x 9½" (6.5cm x 24cm) to the sides of the block and the other two, 17" x 4" (44cm x 10cm) to the top and bottom of the block.

9. Press carefully. Mark the quilting design on the heart and the borders. Do NOT mark the design on the white fabric.

10. Tack together the patchwork, wadding and backing fabric to make a quilt 'sandwich', see 'in a nutshell'.

11. Quilt the marked lines on the heart design, then echo quilt on the white fabric. To do this, quilt a scant ⅛" (3mm) from the edge of the design, repeat in ever decreasing circles until you reach the centre of the piece you are quilting.

12. Quilt the borders.

13. Tack around the finished top and trim, leaving a ¼" (.5cm) seam allowance.

14. Complete the cushion in the Housewife fashion as shown in 'cushion finishes'.

HINTS & TIPS

Basic Sewing Kits: Put these things together in a bag, basket or box and they will always be handy for workshops, holiday breaks etc: Scissors (paper, thread), Pencil, Pen, Sharpener, Eraser, Needles, Pins, Thimble, Threads.

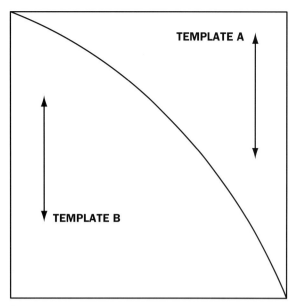

TEMPLATE A

TEMPLATE B

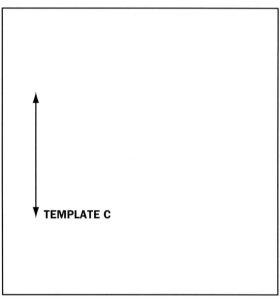

TEMPLATE C

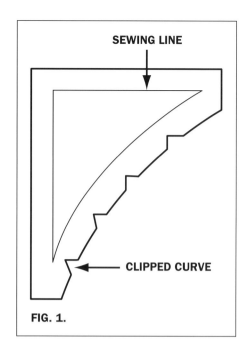

SEWING LINE

CLIPPED CURVE

FIG. 1.

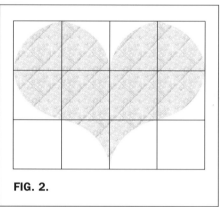

FIG. 2.

THE SOLID LINE IS THE SEWING LINE.
DRAW AROUND THE TEMPLATE ONTO
THE FABRIC, THEN ADD ¼" (.5CM)
SEAM ALLOWANCE WHEN CUTTING
OUT THE PIECES.

HINTS & TIPS

When using a sewing machine, raise it a few inches to ease the strain on your back. I use two bricks wrapped in several layers of newspaper, then 2 layers of brown paper.

hare appliqué

This hare design comes from a medieval tile found in a church. The hare seems really alive and leaps across the cushion. In order to emphasise the hare this cushion is rectangular, so you will need to make a special cushion pad, but you will find the result well worth it.

REQUIREMENTS

Finished Size: 17" x 12"
(45cm x 30cm)

- ½ yard (.5m) background fabric
- ¼ yard (.25m) fabric for hare
- Matching thread for appliqué
- Bias binding

- 2 yards (2m) lace 3" (8cm) wide
- Piece wadding 20" x 15" (50cm x 38cm)
- Backing fabric for quilting 20" x 15" (50cm x 38cm)
- 1 Black bead for eye

TO MAKE: hare appliqué

1. Trace the hare design on to grease proof paper, stick it onto a piece of cereal box card and carefully cut it out.

2. Place the hare right side down onto your chosen fabric and draw around the shape using a sharp pencil. Cut out the hare leaving a ¼" (.5cm) seam allowance.

3. Cut a piece of background fabric 17" x 12" and fold it into quarters to find the centre. Place the hare centrally and pin and tack into place.

4. Appliqué into place, see 'in a nutshell'.

5. Sandwich together the three layers for quilting as described in 'in a nutshell'.

6. Quilt one line close to the hare, then another ¼" (.5cm) away and another ¼" (.5cm) away from that see Fig. 1.

7. Tack all around the edge of the background fabric and trim the wadding and backing to the same size as the background. Add the bead 'eye'.

8. Pin and tack the lace onto the cushion top, two strips down each side and them top and bottom. Mitre the corners of the lace. You may find you need to attach the lace here and there along the free edge.

9. Cut two pieces of backing fabric 12" x 12" (30cm x 30cm). Hem down one edge of each piece.

10. Place the hare right side down and place the two pieces on the back right side up.

11. Bind the cushion with bias binding, taking ¼" (.5cm) seam allowance.

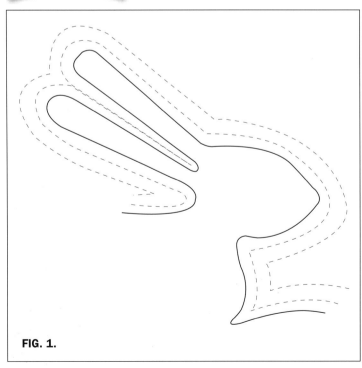

FIG. 1.

14

15

When you are hand piecing, it helps to have an iron handy to piece the seams. Make an 'ironing board' from a thickly folded double sheet. A travel iron is marvellous – some are even available with steam. The sheet and iron combined make an ideal workstation by your chair.

THE SOLID LINE IS THE SEWING LINE. DRAW AROUND THE TEMPLATE ONTO THE FABRIC, THEN ADD ¼" (.5CM) SEAM ALLOWANCE WHEN CUTTING OUT THE PIECES.

TEMPLATE A

16

cathedral *window*

This Cathedral Window cushion is very attractive and although it is fairly time consuming to sew, would make a delightful present – perhaps for a wedding?

REQUIREMENTS

Finished Size: 16" (41cm) square

- ½ yard (.5m) pink fabric
- 1 yard (1 metre) plain blue fabric
- ¼ yard (.25m) multi print fabric (pink and blue)
- ¼ yard (.25m) fabric with roses
- Matching thread
- 16" (41cm) square cushion pad

TO MAKE: cathedral *window*

1. Cut 9 x 7" (18cm) squares in the pink fabric.

2. Cut 16 x 7" (18cm) squares in plain blue.

3. Fold each square in half and, taking a ¼" (.5cm) seam allowance, sew down each end. Fig. 1.

4. Pull the unsewn edges apart and refold the square the other way. Pin as shown. Fig. 2.

5. Sew along the lines shown.

6. Turn the square to the right side, and taking two small stitches, sew the gap in the centre of the square. Fig. 2A. Bring the four corners to the centre of the square and stitch them neatly and firmly to the centre. Repeat with all the squares.

7. Place two prepared squares right sides together and oversew them together along one edge. Fig. 3.

8. Sew all the squares together in the layout shown at Fig. 4.

9. Now cut your insert squares as follows:

- 18 x 2¾" (4.5cm) squares in the pink flowery fabric

- 16 x 2¾" (4.5cm) squares in the pink fabric

- 16 x 2¾" (4.5cm) squares in the rosy fabric

10. Place a 2¾" (4.5cm) square across the seam line as shown in Fig. 5. and pin into place. If you prefer, you can place all the squares into position and tack them into place.

11. Gently pull a folded edge over the square, Fig. 6. and neatly slip stitch it down. Repeat on the opposite side and then the other two sides. Do this until all the complete squares are in place. At the edges, you only need to sew two sides. Fig. 7.

12. Tack all around the edge of the cushion and trim leaving a ¼" (.5cm) seam allowance all round.

In this case I have finished the cushion with piping, but you can choose – see 'cushion finishes'.

HINTS & TIPS

Store the pieces for each block or project in a plastic bag – the self seal ones are ideal. You can pick up the bag at any time and take it and your basic sewing kit with you. It's amazing how much you can do when waiting for appointments etc. The plastic bags can be recycled for more projects too!

18

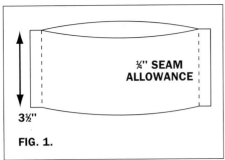

¼" SEAM ALLOWANCE

3½"

FIG. 1.

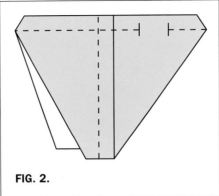
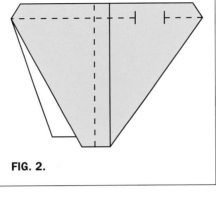

FIG. 2.

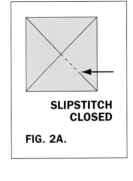

SLIPSTITCH CLOSED

FIG. 2A.

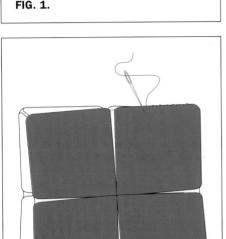

FIG. 3.

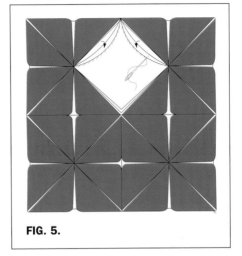

FIG. 5.

HINTS & TIPS

Keep your templates in an envelope or plastic bag with the name of the block on the outside. Tape or staple each packet on a piece of card and keep them in a loose leaf file, then they are always available.

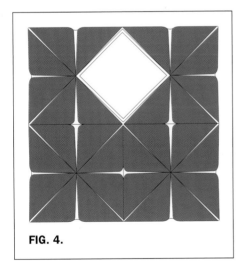

FIG. 4.

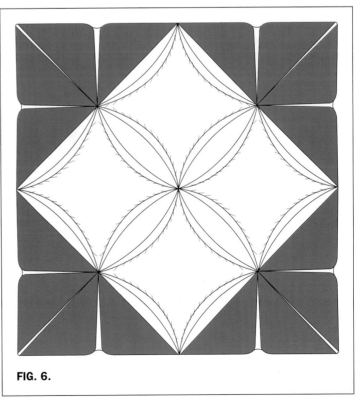

FIG. 6.

grape basket

This is an old traditional design that lends itself to striking colour combinations, as in this example. The colours were chosen from the background fabric in this instance. This cushion has been plainly quilted, but you could always quilt, or even appliqué a bunch of grapes across the basket.

REQUIREMENTS

Finished Size: 16" (41cm) square

- ½ yard (.5m) patterned fabric for corners and backing
- ¼ yard (.25m) of three fabrics (light, medium and dark) for basket
- ¼ yard (.25m) accent fabric (in this case bright pink)

- 16" (41cm) cushion pad
- 18" (46cm) square of 2oz. wadding
- 18" (46cm) square of fabric for backing the quilting
- Matching thread for sewing
- Quilting thread

HINTS & TIPS

Grey thread is a useful colour when piecing fabrics of different colours since it will blend with most colours. It will save you changing threads all the time.

TO MAKE: grape basket

1. Make your templates A, B, C and D in card or template plastic as shown in 'in a nutshell'.

2. From the darker fabric cut 13 x A and 1 x B.

3. From the medium fabric cut 1 x B and 9 x C.

4. From the lighter fabric cut 6 x A, 1 x B, 2 x D and 1 x C.

5. Cut 4 strips 14" (36cm) x 1" (2.5cm) from the accent fabric and lay them to one side.

6. Cut 4 triangles from the background fabric for the edges using Template E.

7. Piece the basket block following Fig. 1.

8. Fold the accent fabric in half lengthways and pin and tack to the block raw edges together Fig. 2.

9. Place the long edge of the background corner on top of the accent fabric and pin and sew into place.

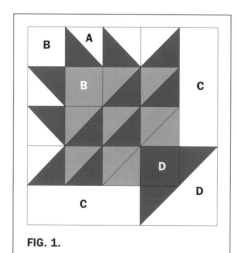

FIG. 1.

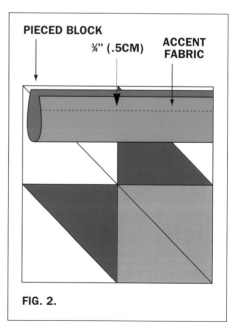

PIECED BLOCK
¼" (.5CM)
ACCENT FABRIC

FIG. 2.

10. Sandwich the layers together for quilting, see 'in a nutshell' and quilt as desired or as shown in Fig. 3.

11. Finish the cushion in the Housewife fashion as shown in 'cushion finishes'.

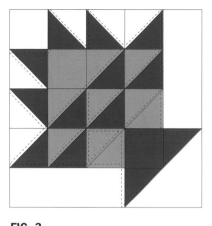

FIG. 3.

THE SOLID LINE IS THE SEWING LINE. DRAW AROUND THE TEMPLATE ONTO THE FABRIC, THEN ADD ¼" (.5CM) SEAM ALLOWANCE WHEN CUTTING OUT THE PIECES.

TEMPLATE C

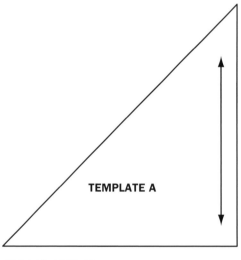

TEMPLATE A

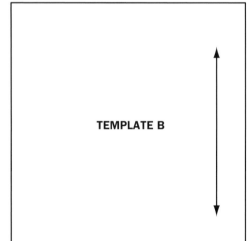

TEMPLATE B

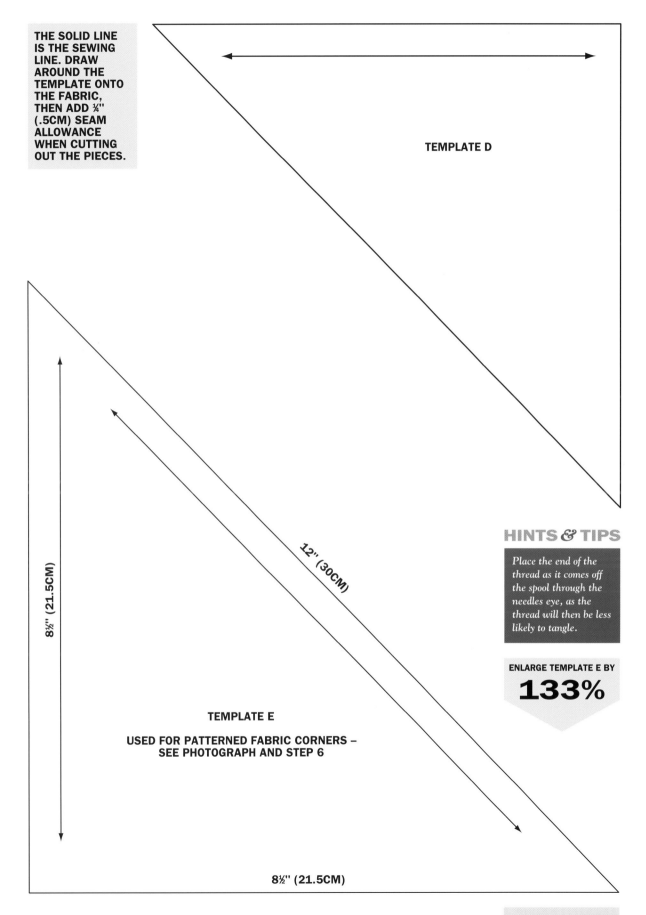

THE SOLID LINE IS THE SEWING LINE. DRAW AROUND THE TEMPLATE ONTO THE FABRIC, THEN ADD ¼" (.5CM) SEAM ALLOWANCE WHEN CUTTING OUT THE PIECES.

TEMPLATE D

8½" (21.5CM)

12" (30CM)

TEMPLATE E

USED FOR PATTERNED FABRIC CORNERS –
SEE PHOTOGRAPH AND STEP 6

8½" (21.5CM)

HINTS & TIPS

Place the end of the thread as it comes off the spool through the needles eye, as the thread will then be less likely to tangle.

ENLARGE TEMPLATE E BY

133%

whole cloth
quilted cushion

Despite all the wonderful colours, patterns and shapes that can be explored when you make patchwork, there is still something lovely about the soft, gentle lines formed by the shadows falling on a piece of fine quilting. A cushion quilted in a soft colour will make a lovely present at any time for anyone of any age and the range of designs you can use for quilting is endless. You can follow the quilters of yesterday and copy their designs, gleaned from nature and the things around them, or look at modern inspiration – architecture for instance. I obtained this design from a piece of wrought iron work – an excellent design source.

REQUIREMENTS

Finished Size: 16" (41cm) square

- ½ yard (.5m) plain fabric (glazed cotton is attractive)
- 18" (46cm) square 2oz. wadding
- 18" (46cm) square butter muslin or quilting backing fabric
- Matching sewing and quilting thread
- 2 yards (2m) fairly fine piping cord
- Water erasable felt pen OR colouring pencil a shade or two darker than the fabric
- 16" (41cm) cushion pad

TO MAKE: whole cloth *quilted cushion*

HINTS & TIPS

One side of the needle has a larger eye than the other. Try both when you have trouble threading.

1. Enlarge the quilting design by 140% on a photocopier, then enlarge the copy by 140%, finally enlarge the second copy by 107%.

2. Cut two 16½" (42cm) squares of fabric. Press one well, fold it into four and finger press the folds. (The other piece will be used for the backing) Tape it to a flat surface with masking tape. Place the design with the + marked on the centre of the folds, and tape the design into place.

3. Trace the design using the water erasable marker or colouring pencil. If you have difficulty seeing the design to trace it, tape the design to a window with the fabric on top and use the Sun as a light-box.

4. Sandwich together the marked top, the wadding and the backing fabric and tack together as shown in 'in a nutshell'.

5. Using small running stitches and following the directions in 'in a nutshell'

quilt along all the marked lines, working from the centre out.

6. When all the quilting is done, tack around the edge of the quilted top and trim the wadding and backing back to the edge. Remove the previous tacking. If you used water erasable marker, wet the quilting to remove it.

7. Finish in the Housewife style right sides together with the front taking ½" seam allowance.

8. Sew a line ¼" from the edge in the Oxford style. Insert the cushion pad.

TEMPLATE A

26

dartmeet

This block is, like many others, the result of a doodle I made one day. The darts are obvious, and since they meet in the middle of the block, I called it Dartmeet, which also happens to be the name of a beauty spot in Devon. I chose these attractive Dutch fabrics because they are rugged and masculine and blend so well together.

REQUIREMENTS

Finished Size: 18" x 18" (46cm x 46cm) square

- ½ yard (.5m) of checked fabric 1
- ¾ yard (.75m) of checked fabric 2
- ¼ yard (.25m) each of two plain fabrics
- ¼ yard (.25m) of butter muslin or quilting backing fabric
- 1 x 19" (48cm) square of 2oz. wadding
- 1 x 18" (46cm) square cushion pad
- Matching thread for sewing and quilting

TO MAKE: dartmeet

1. Cut 4 strips of checked fabric 19" (48cm) x 1" (2.5cm) for the binding and lay to one side.

2. Cut 4 strips of checked fabric 2-29" x 3½" (74cm x 9cm) for the borders and two pieces 19" x 12½" (48cm x 32cm) for the backing.

3. Make your templates as described in 'in a nutshell'.

4. Following the piecing breakdown, Fig. 1. piece your block carefully. It is easier to do this one quarter of the block at a time and then sew the quarters into halves and then the halves together.

5. Fold the border pieces in half and mark a, the halfway point and b, 6" (15cm) both left and right of the centre mark.
   Pin and sew each border into place matching the halfway point with ^ on the block, and the other two points with the edges of the block. This will help keep the seam flat, and prevent distortion of the block.

6. Mitre the corners of the borders, see 'in a nutshell'.

7. Sandwich the layers of quilt top, wadding and quilt backing fabric together as described in 'in a nutshell'.

8. Machine or hand quilt along the lines shown in Fig. 2.

9. Tack around the edge of the cushion top and trim the wadding and backing.

10. Hem down one long edge of each of the backing pieces.

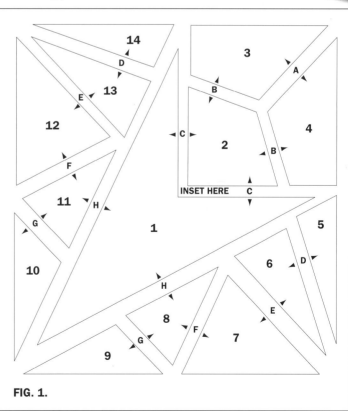

FIG. 1.

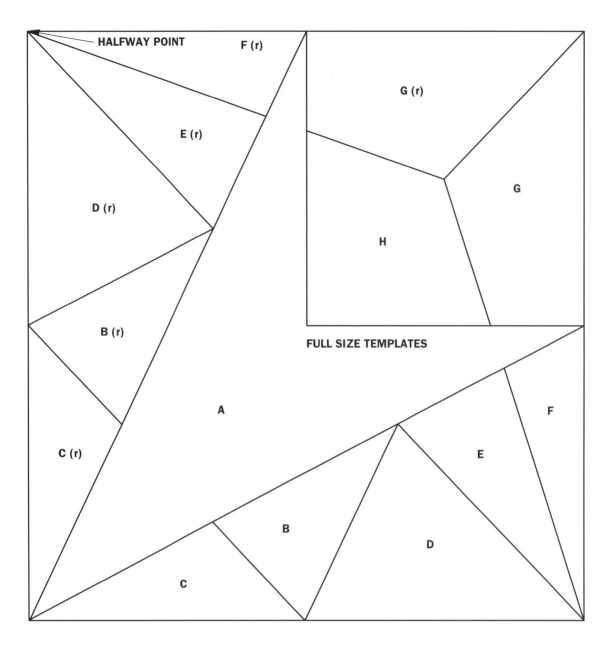

HALFWAY POINT

F (r)

E (r)

D (r)

B (r)

C (r)

A

G (r)

G

H

FULL SIZE TEMPLATES

F

E

D

B

C

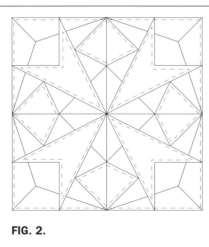

FIG. 2.

11. Place the completed block face down and the two backing piece right sides up on top. Tack around all four edges.

12. Bind the completed cushion top with the strips laid aside earlier.

THE SOLID LINE IS THE SEWING LINE. DRAW AROUND THE TEMPLATE ONTO THE FABRIC, THEN ADD ¼" (.5CM) SEAM ALLOWANCE WHEN CUTTING OUT THE PIECES.

29

jacob's ladder

This is a very old quilt block designed, inspired so legend has it, by the story of Jacob's ladder stretching up to Heaven as told in the Bible. It is a simple design which looks quite complicated, and it looks very nice when lots of blocks are used in a full size quilt. Try photocopying the design several times, cut out the blocks and play with them. You'll be amazed how many arrangements are possible.

REQUIREMENTS

Finished Size: 16" (41cm) square

- ¾ yard green fabric (1) for parts of the block, the borders and backing
- ¼ yard (.25m) each of terracotta (2), light terracotta (3) and patterned (4) fabrics.
- 1 x 16" (41cm) cushion pad

- 18" (46cm) square of 2oz wadding
- 18" (46cm) square of butter muslin or quilting backing fabric
- Thread for sewing
- Gold thread for quilting

TO MAKE: jacob's ladder

1. Make Templates A and B in card or plastic as described in 'in a nutshell'.

2. Cut as follows, leaving ¼" (.5cm) seam allowance on all pieces:

- 10 x Template A in 2
- 10 x Template A in 1
- 4 x Template B in 4
- 4 x Template B in 3

3. Following Fig. 1. and 'in a nutshell' piece the block together.

4. Cut 2 strips of fabric 1-2½" x 16½" (6.5cm x 42cm) and 2 strips 2½" x 12½" (6.5cm x 32cm) for the borders.

5. Press the completed block then sew the two shorter border pieces to two sides of the block, then the longer pieces to the top and bottom.

6. Press the top and sandwich together with the wadding and quilting backing fabric.

7. Outline quilt all the pieces by quilting approximately ¼" (.5cm) from the seam lines. Fig. 2.

8. Finish in the Housewife fashion as shown in 'cushion finishes'.

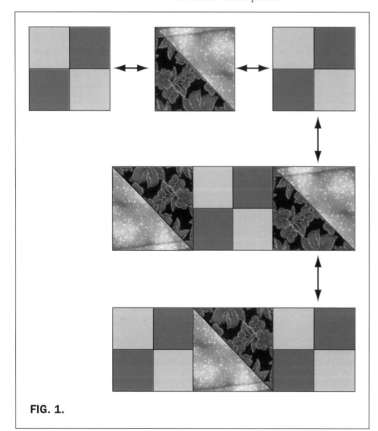

FIG. 1.

30

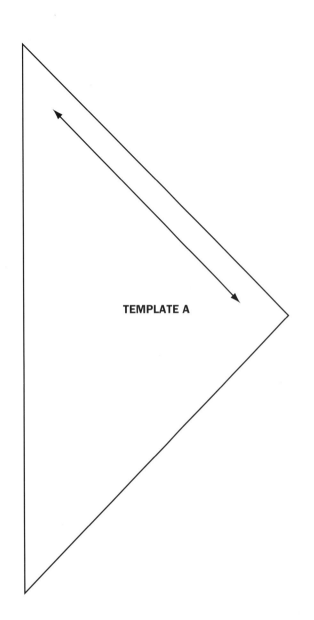

TEMPLATE A

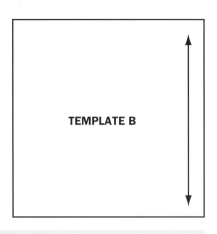

TEMPLATE B

THE SOLID LINE IS THE SEWING LINE. DRAW AROUND THE TEMPLATE ONTO THE FABRIC, THEN ADD ¼'' (.5CM) SEAM ALLOWANCE WHEN CUTTING OUT THE PIECES.

HINTS & TIPS

Before you wash your fabrics, cut a snip off two diagonal corners. This will help prevent the fabric unravelling in the wash.

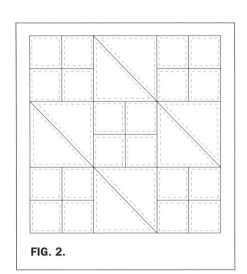

FIG. 2.

hexagon *wreath*

I saw this design several years ago in the centre of a cot quilt. The colours used then were bright orange, yellow and lime green on an avocado green background – very 1970's! It occurred to me that the design would be lovely in other colours and I filed the rough sketch away until recently. A purchase of some 1930 fabric style reprints needed a nice design and so I married the sketch and fabric and am quite pleased with the results! I hope you like it too!

REQUIREMENTS

Finished Size: 18" (46cm) square

- Scraps of fabrics in pastel shades – I used approx. ⅛ yard (.125m) of each of 7 fabrics

- NB – you should choose yellow as one of these fabrics for the centres of the flowers

- ¾ yard (.75m) plain fabric for background and backing

- ¼ yard (.25m) green fabric for the wreath and the binding

- 19" (48cm) square of 2oz. wadding

- 19" (48cm) square of quilting backing fabric or butter muslin

- Cream quilting and sewing thread

TO MAKE: hexagon *wreath*

1. Make your two hexagon templates from cereal box card or template plastic as shown in 'in a nutshell'.

2. Cut 56 paper hexagons using template A and 7 paper hexagons using Template B.

3. Cut 8 fabric hexagons in each colour for piece A leaving a ¼" (.5cm) seam allowance around each and 1 fabric hexagon in each colour from Template B, again leaving the seam allowance.

4. Following the instructions in 'in a nutshell', tack the fabric around all the papers, then make 8 'rosettes' of the A pieces and one 'rosette' of the B pieces.

5. Cut 4 strips of green fabric 19" (48cm) x 1" (2.5cm) for the binding and lay to one side. Cut 8 strips of fabric 1" (2.5cm) wide x 2½" (6.5cm) long for the wreath.

6. Cut an 18" (46cm) square of the plain backing fabric, press it and fold it into four. Open out the fabric and using compasses, with the point on the centre of the fold, mark a 12" (30cm) circle on the fabric.

7. Using the fold lines as a guide, place the first four A rosettes in position and pin them into place, add the other four. When you are happy with the placement, tack the rosettes into place with two or three stitches in the centre hexagon.

8. Fold a green fabric strip in half and place it onto the drawn wreath line, leaving a ¼" (.5cm) seam allowance. Fig. 1.

9. Using running stitch and the occasional back-stitch, sew the strip in place.

10. Now fold the strip over the stitched line and invisibly hem it into place. Fig. 2. Repeat with all the other strips, tucking the ends of the strips under the rosettes.

11. Invisibly hem down all the rosette edges.

12. Place the B rosette over the centre folds and pin and hem into position.

13. Press the finished top, then sandwich it together with the wadding and the quilting backing.

HINTS & TIPS

Wash your fabrics and dry them in a tumble dryer. They then will be unlikely to shrink or run. Also be prepared to wash the project when you have finished it. Constant handling whilst piecing and quilting can leave your work greasy with hand oils. A wash will refresh it, particularly if you intend to give it to someone as a gift.

14. Quilt around all the rosettes and wreath strips, close to the edges. Tack around the background square and trim the wadding and backing flush with the edge.

15. Lay the finished top flat. Cut two pieces of fabric 18" x 12" (46cm x 30cm) and hem down one long side of each. Lay these right sides up on the quilted top and tack all the layers together.

16. Bind the cushion using the green strips laid to one side.

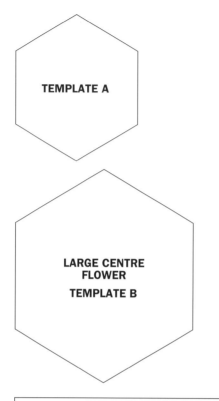

TEMPLATE A

LARGE CENTRE
FLOWER

TEMPLATE B

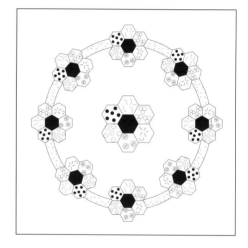

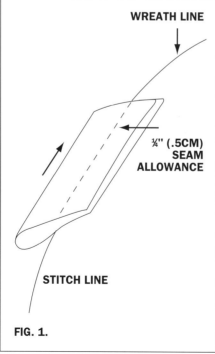

WREATH LINE

¼" (.5CM)
SEAM
ALLOWANCE

STITCH LINE

FIG. 1.

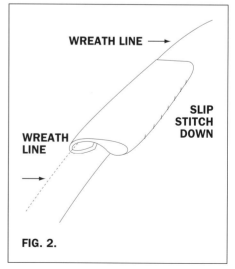

WREATH LINE

SLIP
STITCH
DOWN

WREATH
LINE

FIG. 2.

hawaiian *appliqué cushion*

This appliqué technique originated in Hawaii. It is said that missionaries visiting the island introduced sewing to the native women, though it is thought that these designs and this technique belong firmly to the imagination of the South Seas women and the influence of the flora in that region. The design is made by folding paper into eight layers and cutting intricate motifs to give a strong coloured image which is then appliquéd to a larger piece of fabric. Usually only two colours are used. Once the design is appliquéd into place, the maker will 'echo' or 'wave' quilt around the design at ¼" (.25cm) intervals to the edge of the quilt. For this cushion, I only folded the paper into four and cut a simple design, but you could develop a challenging design with more folds and a more intricate motif.

REQUIREMENTS

Finished Size: 16" (41cm) square

- ¾ yard (.75m) darker fabric
- ½ yard (.5m) lighter fabric
- ¼ yard (.25m) muslin or quilting backing fabric
- 18" (46cm) square 2oz. wadding
- Matching thread for sewing and quilting

HINTS & TIPS

Use a polystyrene ceiling tile – stuck to a board if possible – to which to pin your block pieces. As you piece each seam, replace it on the block, so you don't lose your way, particularly when piecing a block with lots of pieces.

TO MAKE: hawaiian *appliqué cushion*

1. Enlarge Template A by 140%.

2. Stick the design to cereal box card and carefully cut it out.

3. Draw around the design on the wrong side of the lighter fabric and cut it out leaving a ¼" (.5cm) seam allowance.

4. Cut a 14" (35cm) square of darker fabric, press it, fold it into four and finger press the folds. Open it out again and lay it flat. Place the appliqué design centrally using the folds as a guide. Pin and tack it into place, with the tacking stitches being ½" (1.5cm) away from the design edge.

5. Appliqué the motif into place using matching thread and turning approx. ⅛" (.25cm) under as you go. Take tiny invisible hemming stitches. You may need to clip into the seam allowances on the curves. Also see 'in a nutshell'.

6. When the motif is fully stitched down, sandwich the top, wadding and quilting backing fabric.

7. Quilt over the motif and the background by echoing the design in lines ¼" (.25cm) apart. Fig. 2. Tack around the finished top and trim the backing and wadding to the same size as the cushion top.

8. From the paler fabric cut two strips 2½" x 14" (6.5cm x 35cm) and two strips 2½" x 17 (6.5cm x 43cm).

9. Taking a ¼" (.25cm) seam allowance, sew the shorter strips to two sides of the block, then the longer pieces to the other two sides.

10. Using the darker fabric for the back, finish the cushion in the Housewife style as shown in 'cushion finishes'.

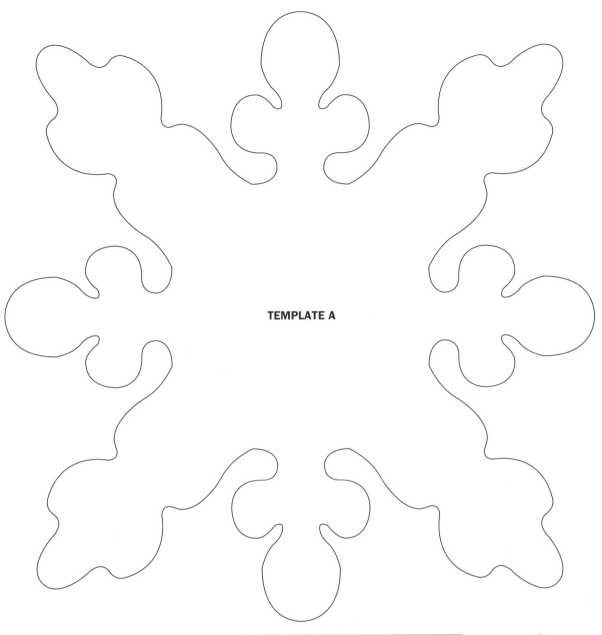

TEMPLATE A

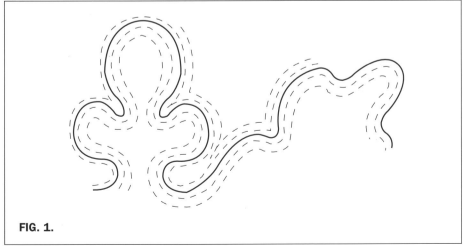

FIG. 1.

ENLARGE TEMPLATE A BY
140%

grandma and *grandpa bear*

Here's a chance to make these delightful bear cushions and learn a new technique at the same time. Shadow trapunto is an easy and versatile technique which once mastered can be used on many applications. It is ideal for adding colour to small areas such as collars and cuffs and dress bodices, since it can be hand washed.

Trapunto means 'stuffing' and the technique requires you to 'stuff' the quilting after it is completed. The colour comes from embroidery silks or wools which are used for 'stuffing' – so save all your odds and ends!

REQUIREMENTS

Finished Size: 18" (46cm) square

- ½ yard (.5m) each of two fabrics for borders and backing
- ½ yard (.5m) ivory batiste, voile or other sheer fabric 60" (140cm) wide (see suppliers)
- 1 x 12" (30cm) square 2oz wadding (split apart to make two thinner wadding layers)
- 2 x 18" (46cm) cushion pads
- Matching thread
- Assortment of wools and embroidery silks for trapunto*
- Tapestry needle
- Medium dark blue quilting thread
- Gold thread for glasses
- Heart button for Grandma's collar

TO MAKE: grandma and *grandpa bear*

1. Cut four pieces batiste 11" (28cm) square. Lay two aside for other cushion.

2. Enlarge the designs by 107% for Grandma and 102% for Grandpa. Lightly trace the Grandma design onto the batiste, then tack the wadding between the two layers of batiste, making a quilt 'sandwich', see 'in a nutshell'.

3. Using the blue quilting thread, quilt along all the marked lines.

4. Work the trapunto – see page 40.

5. Embroider the eyes and nose in place using embroidery silk and stem stitch.

Use the design as a guide.

6. Add the button to Grandma's collar.

7. From the border fabrics, cut 4 strips 21" x 4½" (53cm x 12cm) for each cushion top.

8. Taking a ¼" (.5cm) seam allowance, sew the borders into place, mitring the corners as shown in 'in a nutshell'.

9. Finish the cushion in the Housewife fashion as shown in 'cushion finishes'.

HINTS & TIPS

Store a piece of quilting in progress in a pillow case.

* Experiment to choose the right colours for your design. I used a fairly bright mid brown for the bear 'fur' and a bright blue for Grandma's dress and Grandpa's waistcoat. Bright pink is ideal for the paw pads.

To Work The Trapunto:

Thread the tapestry needle with a double length of yarn. From the back of the design, insert the needle through the bottom layer and wadding, but do not go through the top layer. Try not to run the needle through the wadding as this will cause colour loss. Work the needle through the length of the design leaving approximately $\frac{1}{32}$" (1mm) at the starting point. Cut the yarn close to the fabric, again leaving $\frac{1}{32}$" (1mm) at the finishing point. Fig. 1. Now insert the needle through the back layer only and using the point of the needle, hook or pull the yarn ends inside. Now place another layer of yarn alongside the first and cut it at the other end. Keep the strands parallel. Carry on in this way until the space is filled see Figs. 2 and 3. It is important not to overfill the shapes as the yarn cannot be taken out and the fabric may pucker if the space is overstuffed. Hold the work to the light to see how much yarn is in the design and to see if more stuffing is required. The needle point can be inserted through the top layer of the design to adjust the yarn if necessary.

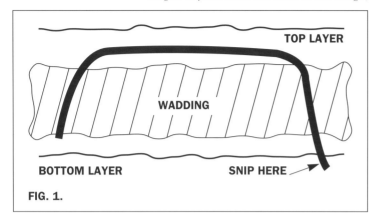

TOP LAYER

WADDING

BOTTOM LAYER

SNIP HERE

FIG. 1.

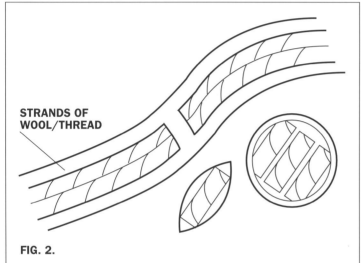

STRANDS OF WOOL/THREAD

FIG. 2.

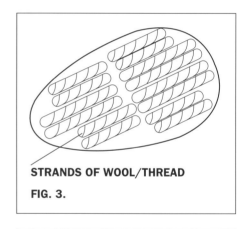

STRANDS OF WOOL/THREAD

FIG. 3.

HINTS & TIPS

Keep chopsticks or plastic swizzle sticks in your workbox – they are great for pushing out corners or stuffing small areas!

TEMPLATE A

41

TEMPLATE B

ENLARGE TEMPLATE B BY
102%

42

desirable *residence*

Take a basic block like this house and go to town! Add embellishments and embroidery details and you can make a desirable residence of your own.

REQUIREMENTS

Finished Size: 18" (46cm) square

- ½ yard (.5m) fabric for backing
- ¼ yard (.25m) green for grass
- ¼ yard (.25m) blue for sky
- Scraps of different coloured fabrics for house, tree trunks, path, door and chimney
- Varied green scraps for trees

- Embroidery silks
- Assorted buttons for flower heads
- Small appliqué motifs for windows
- Scrap of lace for windows
- Buttons, charms, etc. to embellish (see suppliers)

HINTS & TIPS

For neat quilting – practice! practice! practice!

TO MAKE: desirable *residence*

1. Make your templates as shown in 'in a nutshell'.

2. Cut a piece of blue fabric 19" x 12½" (48cm x 32cm) for the sky and a piece of green 19" x 6½" (48cm x 16cm) for the grass.

3. From the templates cut your pieces for the house adding a ¼" (.5cm) seam allowance.

4. Stitch the appliqué motifs into place on the window pieces and add lace down both sides of each window.

5. Piece the house together as in Fig. 1. see 'in a nutshell'. Turn under the ¼" (.5cm) seam allowance and appliqué the house into place on the sky fabric.

6. Appliqué the path into place on the grass fabric.

7. Place the sky and grass fabrics right sides together and sew taking a ¼" (.5cm) seam allowance.

8. Cut two tree trunks, one 7½" x 1" (19cm x 2.5cm) and one 4½" x ¾" (11.5cm x 2cm). Turn under a small hem and pin

and stitch into position each side of the house as shown in Fig. 2.

9. Make Suffolk Puffs for the trees as follows:

- A. Cut 15 x 3" (7.5cm) circles of assorted green fabrics using Template G

- B. Thread your needle with green thread and, using it double, tie the ends together in a knot

- C. Turn in approx. ⅛" (.25cm) to the wrong side and using a running stitch, sew all around the edge of the circle. Pull the thread carefully but firmly and gather up the fabric forming a 'puff'. Take two or three small stitches and fasten off the thread. Pinch the edges of the puff and encourage it to lie flat

- D. Repeat with the other 14 circles

10. Sew the puff into place on the trees taking care to cover up the ends of the tree trunks.

11. Embroider stems and leaves of flowers over the grass as Fig. 2.

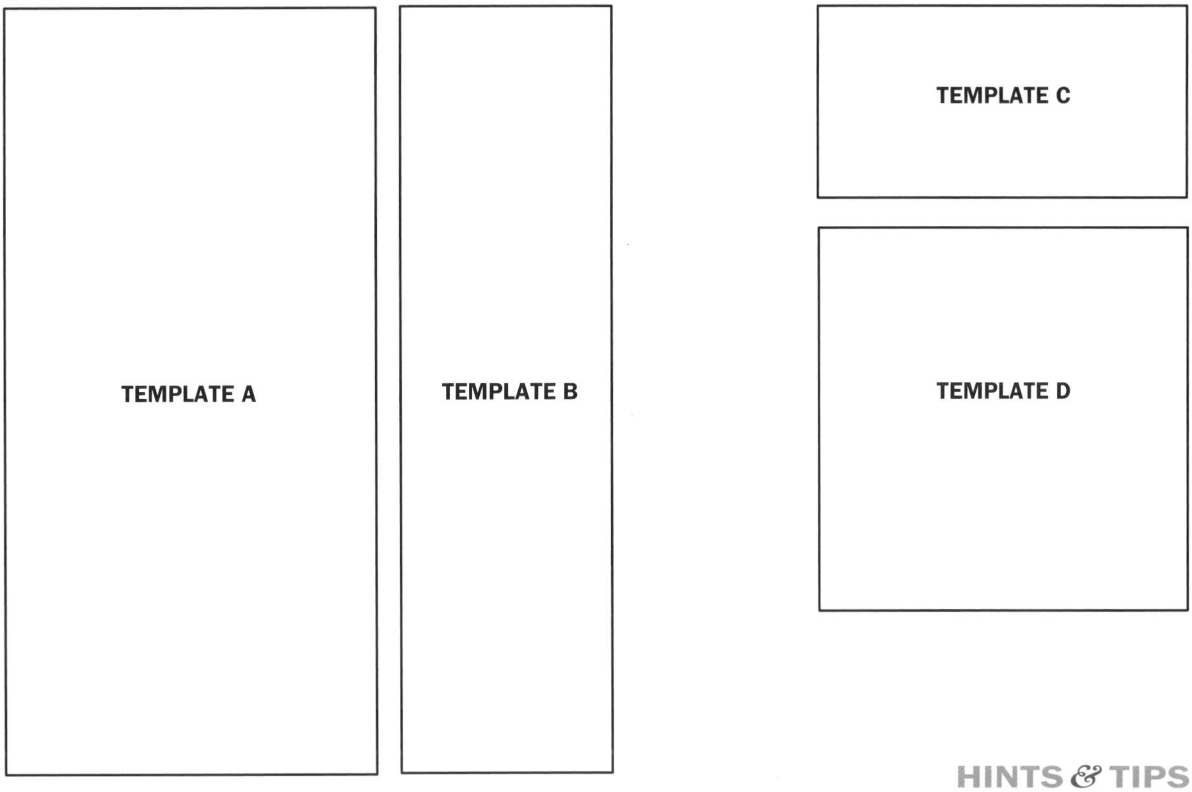

TEMPLATE A

TEMPLATE B

TEMPLATE C

TEMPLATE D

12. Embroider the vine down the wall of the house using lazy daisy stitch (see Stitches).

13. Quilt the cushion top as suggested in Fig. 3.

14. Finish the cushion in the Housewife fashion as shown in 'cushion finishes'.

THE SOLID LINE IS THE SEWING LINE. DRAW AROUND THE TEMPLATE ONTO THE FABRIC, THEN ADD ¼" (.5CM) SEAM ALLOWANCE WHEN CUTTING OUT THE PIECES.

HINTS & TIPS

TEMPLATE E

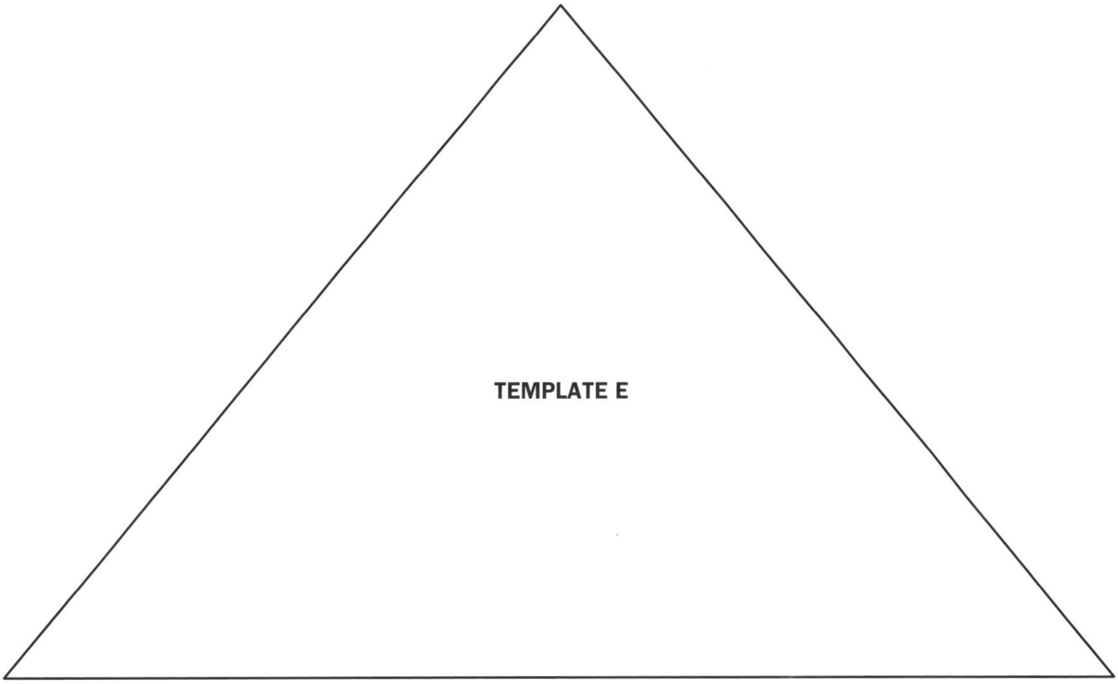

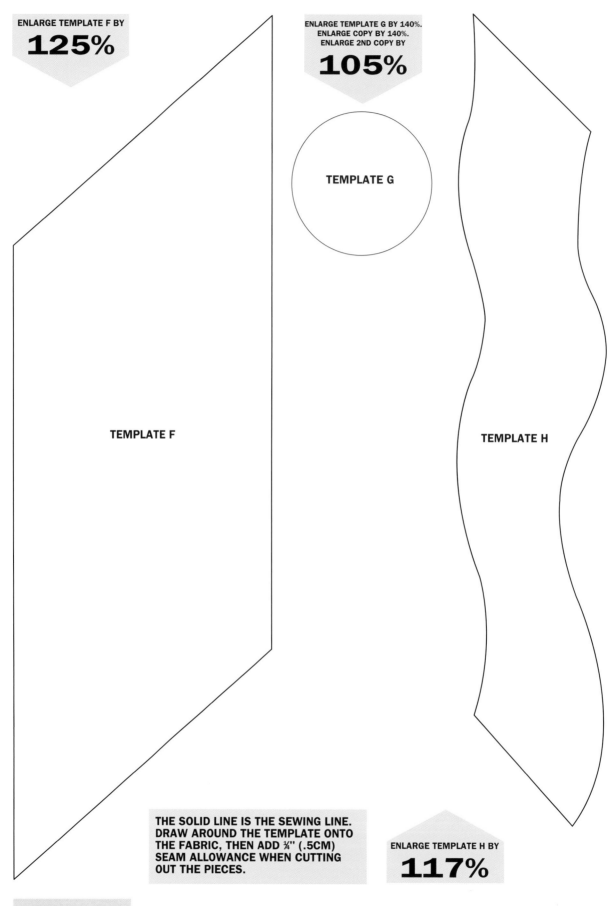

ENLARGE TEMPLATE F BY
125%

ENLARGE TEMPLATE G BY 140%.
ENLARGE COPY BY 140%.
ENLARGE 2ND COPY BY
105%

TEMPLATE G

TEMPLATE F

TEMPLATE H

THE SOLID LINE IS THE SEWING LINE.
DRAW AROUND THE TEMPLATE ONTO
THE FABRIC, THEN ADD ¼'' (.5CM)
SEAM ALLOWANCE WHEN CUTTING
OUT THE PIECES.

ENLARGE TEMPLATE H BY
117%

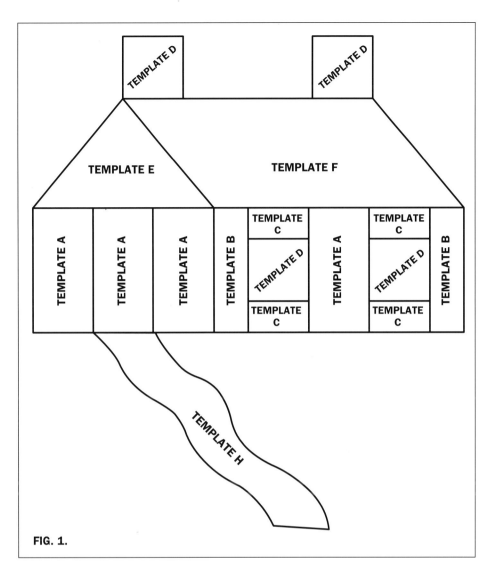

FIG. 1.

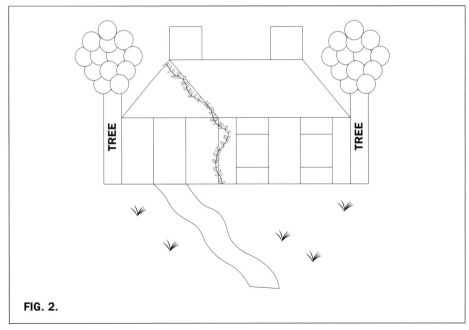

FIG. 2.

47

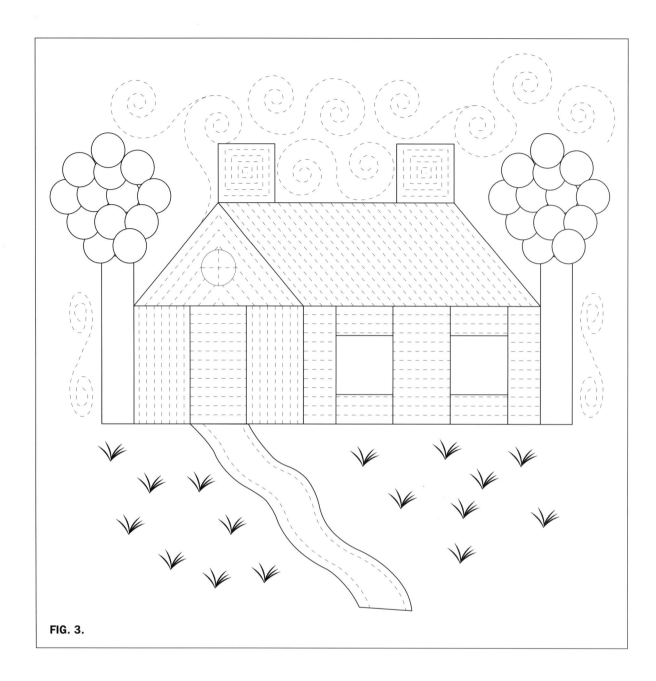

FIG. 3.

happy scraps

This cushion is larger than you would usually expect and is designed for a teenager's room, though it could also be used in the car. I have filled this one with polystyrene beads so it can be sat on or leaned on or whatever. Scraps were used which, chosen with care, could reflect the interests of the recipient.

REQUIREMENTS

Finished Size: 19"x 18" (48cm x 45cm)

- 35 different scraps for patchwork

- 1 yard (1m) denim chambray for strips and backing

- Piece of wadding 24" (60 cm) square

- Grey thread for sewing

- Matching thread for quilting

- 24" (60cm) square of butter muslin to back quilting

TO MAKE: happy scraps

1. Make your templates as outlined in 'in a nutshell'. If you wish to machine piece, add ¼" (.5cm) seam allowance to the template before you cut it. If you wish to hand piece, cut the template to the size given, then add the seam allowance when cutting the fabric.

2. Cut 10 triangles using Template A.

3. Cut 4 strips of chambray 1½" x 8½" (4cm x 21cm) for sashing.

4. Cut 4 strips 2½" x 23" (6cm x 45cm) for borders. Lay the chambray pieces to one side.

5. Sew 5 strips of 7 triangles as shown in Fig. 1.

6. Sew the strips and sashing together as Fig. 1. following numbers 1-9.

7. Sew on the borders top and bottom then each side.

8. Press the completed top.

9. Sandwich together the completed top, wadding and butter muslin, see 'in a nutshell'.

10. Outline quilt the triangles as shown in Fig. 2. Trim the quilted top and machine zig zag around all four sides.

11. Complete the cushion. I found it better to use an 18" (45cm) zip. Insert that as follows:

- A. cut one piece of denim chambray 19" x 20" (48cm x 50cm) for the backing. Zig zag around the four sides to neaten

- B. Taking a ½" (.5cm) seam allowance, sew the backing and top together –

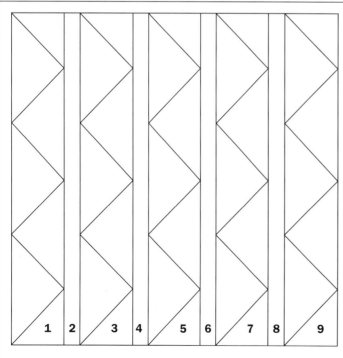

FIG. 1.

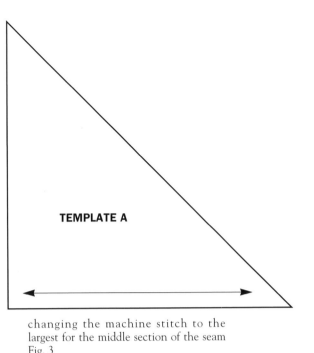

TEMPLATE A

TEMPLATE B

changing the machine stitch to the largest for the middle section of the seam Fig. 3

- C. Place the zip right side down on the seam, and tack into place

- D. Sew the zip into place around all four sides

- E. Unpick the stitches on the right side, revealing the zip sewn into place

- F. With fabrics right sides together, sew around the three remaining sides taking a ½" (.5cm) seam allowance

- G. Turn to right side and push the corners out so they are nice and square

12. Make a cushion pad from strong ticking or cambric and fill as desired with feathers, polyester or polystyrene beads (available from pet shops).

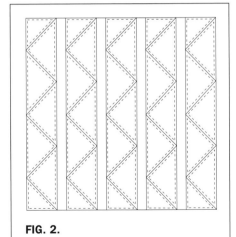

FIG. 2.

THE SOLID LINE IS THE SEWING LINE. DRAW AROUND THE TEMPLATE ONTO THE FABRIC, THEN ADD ¼" (.5CM) SEAM ALLOWANCE WHEN CUTTING OUT THE PIECES.

FIG. 3.

52

sunflower *cushion*

Stencilling is very popular at the moment and is an ideal way to inexpensively decorate walls and furniture, but fabric too can benefit from the treatment. I have used plain muslin fabric, stencilled it with this attractive sunflower, stencil no. 5505 from the StenSource International range available from P&Q (see Suppliers)

REQUIREMENTS

Finished Size: 16" (41cm) square

- ½ yard (.5m) cream cotton muslin fabric (pre-washed is easier to stencil)
- Stencil as described above, though you could use any stencil or cut your own
- Fabric paints: green, yellow and brown
- Medium stencil brush, old saucer and kitchen paper

- Water erasable felt pen (available from quilt shops)
- Brown and yellow quilting thread (I used DMC fine crochet cotton in variegated colours)
- 18" (46cm) square 2oz. wadding
- 18" (46cm) butter muslin or quilting backing fabric
- Cream thread for sewing
- 16" (41cm) cushion pad

TO MAKE: sunflower *cushion*

1. Cut a square of muslin 16½" (42cm) square.

2. Press it well. Fold into four and finger press the folds. Open flat and tape to a flat surface with masking tape.

3. Position the corner piece of the stencil carefully in one corner. Make sure you can position it in the same place on the other three corners, i.e. mark the stencil at the edge of the fabric. Tape the stencil into place. Starting with the green paint, stencil the design as follows (you may want to try on a spare piece of fabric first!):

A. Wet your brush and dry it on paper so it is just damp

B. Dip into the paint and pick up a small amount on the brush. Work the brush on the saucer to load it with paint, then wipe it on the kitchen paper. When there seems to be hardly any paint there it is about right

C. Holding your brush upright, dab the bristles into the stencil, pressing quite firmly and repeating with a tapping motion. Make sure the bristles go right to the edges of the design. Leave the stencil in place for a few moments, then remove the tape, wipe clean the stencil and re-position it in another corner

D. Repeat until all the corners are done

E. Wash the stencil in washing up water, and dry it for further use

F. When the stencil paint is dry, which will be almost immediately, press the fabric on the wrong side with a fairly hot iron to 'set' the design

4. Enlarge the quilting design to 133%

5. Transfer the design to the centre of the stencilled fabric by placing the fabric on top of the design and tracing it through with the water erasable pen. If you have difficulty seeing through the fabric, tape

HINTS & TIPS

Sign and date every piece of your work – even cushions!

53

the design to a window, tape the fabric on to and use the best light source available to man as a light-box!

6. Sandwich together the marked top, the wadding and the quilting backing fabric as shown in 'in a nutshell'.

7. Quilt from the centre out along the brown lines, and finishing with the sunflower petals. Then quilt around the edges of the stencilled motifs using the appropriate colour thread.

8. Tack around the four edges of the quilted piece and trim the wadding and backing back to the fabric edge.

9. Finish the cushion in the Housewife fashion as described in 'cushion finishes'.

10. Wet the cushion top in cold water to remove the water erasable marker.

TEMPLATE A

fans of friendship
pincushions

Finally I have included this rather nice pincushion. Although it is small it is still a cushion, and will always be useful!

HINTS & TIPS

When you wish to trace a quilting design on to your fabric, use your window as a light box. Tape the design to the window, and the fabric on top. Trace the design with your chosen marker.

TO MAKE: fans of friendship *pincushions*

At QUILTS UK in 1993, the organisers were delighted to welcome Aline G. Del'Ve and her party, many of whom are members of the Venice Quilters Guild in Florida, United States of America. Many of the stewards and organisers were surprised and thrilled to be given a Fan pincushion – not least because the theme that year was FANS!

One of the party explained that when the Guild was holding an exhibition, they estimated that there would be approximately 2,000 visitors, so they set to and made 2,000 Fan pincushions. Unfortunately I didn't think to ask how many members their Guild in fact has, but I should imagine everyone was kept busy making so many pincushions! Here is the pattern for you to make your own – or perhaps your local group is holding an Exhibition?!

1. Using template A, cut out 4 pieces, remembering to leave ¼" (.5cm) seam allowances.

2. Piece them together as shown in Fig. 1.

3. If you wish to include lace, slightly gather it and sew it along the curved edge of the pieced blades. See Fig. 2.

4. Cut out Template B in the same fabric as you wish to use for the backing, again remembering to allow ¼" (.5cm) seam allowance.

5. Now carefully pin and sew piece B into place.

6. Cut out template C, again with ¼" (.5cm)

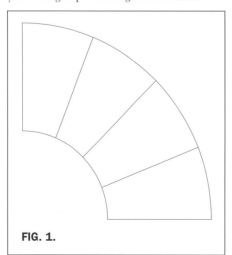

FIG. 1.

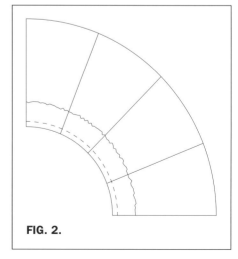

FIG. 2.

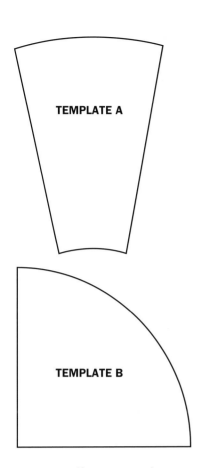

TEMPLATE A

TEMPLATE B

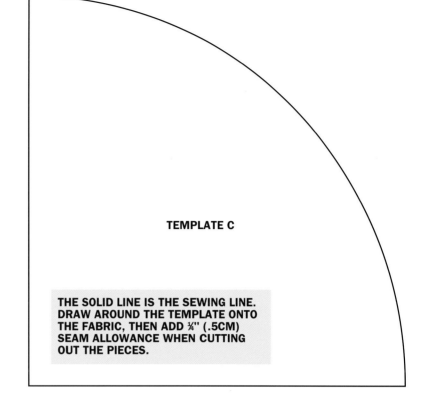

TEMPLATE C

THE SOLID LINE IS THE SEWING LINE.
DRAW AROUND THE TEMPLATE ONTO
THE FABRIC, THEN ADD ¼" (.5CM)
SEAM ALLOWANCE WHEN CUTTING
OUT THE PIECES.

seam allowance, and place it right sides together with the pieced part. Sew around the curved side and one flat side, leaving a space in the other flat side to stuff your pincushion. Turn the piece through to the right side, making sure that the points are nice and sharp (you can use a large knitting needle for that).

5. Stuff your pincushion firmly but evenly, then slipstitch the opening closed.

If you want to make these as presents, you can always put your name, or the name of your group on the back before you sew it all together.

cushion *finishes*

There are many different ways to finish a cushion – the nasty bit at the end when you have created a masterpiece but it is not yet a cushion proper! – and you are best advised to try different methods and find the one you like best. Deirdre Amsden, 'the well-known quilt maker' suggested keeping the fronts from old shirts and using them for the back, since the buttons to fasten it are already in place! An ingenious idea, but not much help if your stock of old shirts is limited. I am listing the methods I use in order of ease – there are many more but these should cover most needs.

HINTS & TIPS

Cut templates in plastic – ice cream tub lids etc, so you can see the fabric through the plastic when placing small motifs etc.

TO MAKE: housewife

Housewife

This system is ideal for most cushions. You will need extra fabric, usually the same as the border or one of the main fabrics in the cushion front.

1. Cut your pieces of fabric.

2. Hem down one long side on each piece. Do this by turning in ¼" (.5cm) (pressing may help) then turning this under again, trapping the raw edge. Hand or machine stitch this turning down.

3. If you wish to bind your cushion, place the cushion top right side down on a flat surface. Place one backing piece right side up on top of this, then the second backing piece on top of that, Fig. 1.

4. Pin and tack all around the cushion top to hold the back in place.

5. Bind as shown in 'Binding' in 'in a nutshell'.
    If you don' t wish to bind the top, place the top wrong side down on a flat surface, and add the two backing pieces wrong sides up. Fig. 2. Taking a ¼" (.5cm) seam allowance, pin, tack and sew the three layers together. Trim the tips of the corners, then turn through to the right side by putting your hand in through the opening and pulling the cushion top through, making sure that the corners are sharp.

If you wish you can close the two backing pieces with press studs, buttons, Velcro etc,

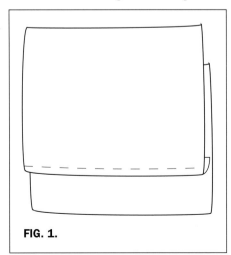

FIG. 1.

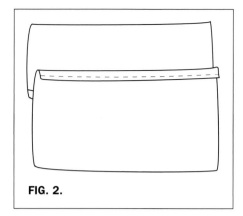

FIG. 2.

though since the pieces are generously cut, there is usually no need.

Oxford

This is a variation on the Housewife method of finishing a cushion. When you have added a border to the main pattern on your cushion front – see the Grandma and Grandpa Shadow Trapunto Cushions – make the border wider so that the whole cushion top is 3" wider than the cushion pad. Join the front and the back of the cushion together in the usual way, but when you have turned it through and pressed it, mark a line lightly in pencil 1½" away from the finished edge. Fig. 3. Machine stitch or quilt along this line. This adds an interesting edge as shown on several examples in this book.

Zip Fastener

This is a good way to use up old zips, as well as being a neat way to finish a cushion. For an 18" cushion cover you would need a 12" zip, for a 16" cushion a 10" zip.

1. Cut a piece of fabric the length of the cushion and the width + 1". Cut the width in half, and zig-zag stitch or pink the raw edges. Place the neatened edges raw sides together and stitch together again using a normal stitch length for the first three inches, a gathering stitch for the length of the zip, and normal stitch length for the remaining three inches. See Fig. 3. on page 51.

2. Press open the seam, and place the zip face down in position. Tack both ends into place. Slightly open the zip. Tack and sew around it and machine stitch into place with a zipper foot (which should come with your machine).

3. Using a seam unpicker or sharp scissors, unpick the seam the length of the zip.

FIG. 3.

This should be easy because you used a long stitch.

4. Place this panel complete with the zip face down right sides together with the cushion front, and, taking a ½" seam allowance, pin, tack and sew the two together. Place your finger in the gap in the zip (this is why you opened it slightly!) and ease the zip down an inch or so, then open it fully.

5. Turn the cushion to the right side, make sure the corners are square and insert your cushion pad.

Interesting Finishes
Piping

This adds a decorative finish to the cushion
.

1. Cut bias * strips 1" (2.5 cm) wide and long enough to go around the cushion with 2" to spare, joining the strip if necessary to make it continuous.

2. Fold the strip around piping cord (available from drapers shops) and sew into position. Fig. 4. leaving 2" or so at each end.

3. Place the raw edges of the finished piping against the raw edge of the cushion top,

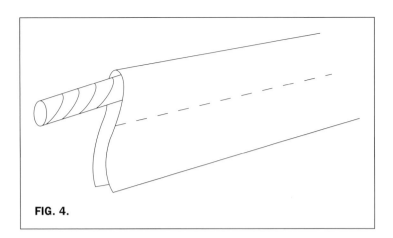

FIG. 4.

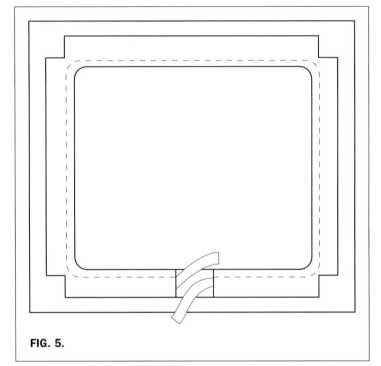

FIG. 5.

B. Fold one end of the piping fabric back on itself and place the other on top, Fig. 6A and B.

C. Tack and sew the join then pin, tack and sew it into place on the cushion top

D. Finish the back of the cushion as you wish

NB It is usually recommended that fabric cut for piping should be on the bias in order to allow for the ease needed to go around corners. However, I have found that straight strips will work well provided the curve is not too severe. It works for cushion piping, and saves a great deal of fabric. If however you prefer to cut your fabric on the bias, or wish to cut a quantity as shown in 'in a nutshell', purchase extra fabric to be sure you don't run out

Cording

Add a touch of style with a corded edge to your cushion. Using a matching thread, and starting in the middle at the bottom of the cushion, simply sew the cord into place. When you get to the join, stitch over the ends of the cord several times, then sew them together neatly.

right sides together and pin and tack into place. When you get to the end, splice the two ends together as follows:

A. Cut the ends of the piping cord straight where they meet and stitch them together, Fig. 6.

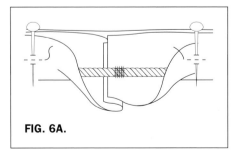

FIG. 6A.

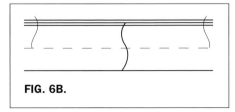

FIG. 6B.

in a nutshell

Each of the projects included in The Patchwork & Quilting Book of Cushions will have instructions and special hints for that particular item, but the essentials of quiltmaking remain basically the same, so this guide to the fundamentals of patchwork, quilting and appliqué is included. Please refer to the article/projection which you are interested for the materials required etc, then use this guide to help you. Read through the information below carefully each time you plan a project, it will help you to avoid making costly and frustrating mistakes.

Understanding projects

The projects include templates wherever necessary, and by and large they need ¼" seam allowance. Should this be different you will be told. The template will have a solid line (the cutting line). These templates should be traced and either stuck to a piece of card; or traced onto template plastic (available from quilting suppliers) then accurately cut out — a craft knife is usually best for this. Be sure to mark them with the size and number of the template together with the project name.

Where measurements are given for borders, they will usually include the ¼" seam allowance, but check the project information. Templates for appliqué do not usually have seam allowances included.

Fabrics

Carefully check the yardage amounts given in your chosen project. Cotton fabrics are the best and easiest to work with and the widths available are usually 44/45" wide, but this is not always the case. It is worth getting into the habit of washing your fabrics when you purchase them so that any colour running or shrinkage problems will be reduced. It will also make the fabric softer and nicer to handle.

Marking

Should you be machine piecing and cutting your pieces with a rotary cutter, there will be no need to mark any lines on your fabrics, but you should choose with care the marking used for hand piecing.

A hard pencil kept very sharp works well, and you should run it consistently around the template edges, making sure that you have placed template along the grain line as shown in your chosen project, and that you are marking the WRONG side of the fabric. Strips of sandpaper stuck to the underside of the template will help to prevent it shifting as you try to draw around it. All pieces to be hand sewn must have ¼" seam allowance added at the cutting stage. There are various ways to mark this line, from a brass wheel to a quilters' quarter, but confidence soon builds sufficiently for you to judge the allowance by eye. Cut out sufficient pieces to make a sample block, and make it up first to be sure that the pieces are accurate; that you haven't given yourself too many bias edges; and that the block comes to the correct size when carefully pressed. When you are satisfied, carry on and cut out the pieces for the entire project.

Piecing

When machine piecing, make sure that you have a ¼" guide to ensure accuracy. If your presser foot is not exactly ¼" try asking your local parts stockist if there is a patchwork foot for your machine, or ask your local quilting supplies shop. Failing that, mark an accurate guide on the throat plate of your machine with masking tape. Adding several layers will actually give you a raised edge to butt the fabric against, which can be a great help. Sew along the entire length of the pieces. When hand piecing, remember that your marked line is your sewing line, and that you must ONLY sew along its length, not into the seam allowance. Place a pin at either end of the line you are going to sew, and, starting with a backstitch sew along the line with running stitch taking an occasional backstitch to add strength. Take a couple of backstitches at the end of the line.

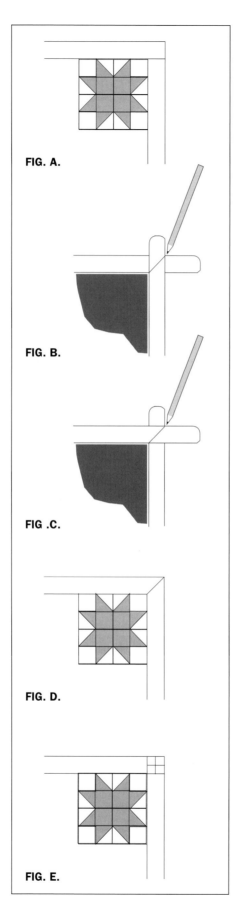

FIG. A.

FIG. B.

FIG .C.

FIG. D.

FIG. E.

English Piecing

This is the name given to piecing over papers. In this instance the smaller template of the two usually given in such a project i.e. the one without seam allowance is the actual size, and you use this one to cut out your papers. These should be made of stiff paper, and it is very important that they should be accurate. Now use the larger template to cut your fabrics. Place the paper in the centre of the fabric and turning the seam allowance over the edge of the paper tack it into place (see Fig. J. in box), starting with a knot in the thread and ending with a backstitch. Once all the pieces have been tacked, oversew them together neatly along each edge.

Appliqué

There are several ways to apply applique. For machine applique, either use Bondaweb® to iron the pieces into place, followed by satin stitch around the piece, or use a decorative button-hole type stitch to attach and decorate in one go. The notes on machine applique projects will go into more detail.

For hand applique, mark your design lightly on the right side of your fabric, and then pin or tack the pieces onto the background up in the order that they should be stitched. Sew them into place using either a) a blind hemming stitch or b) buttonhole stitch, taking care not to turn order or applique any edges that will lie under the other applique pieces.

Pressing

Most projects will need to be pressed several times during their production with the possible exception of silk and velvet pieces. Wherever possible seams should be pressed to one side, and preferably the darker side or away from the area which is to be quilted. Aggressive use of a steam iron can stretch the fabric badly, especially along bias edges, so it is important to either use a dry iron or press rather than iron your work, All the parts of a quilt e.g. top, sashing, borders should be pressed before it is assembled, and again before sandwiching ready for quilting.

Assembling A Quilt Top

Once you have finished all your quilt blocks, lay them out on a flat surface and join them first into rows of the required length, then join the rows, using a ¼" seam allowance throughout. Now add your borders – first the top and bottom then the two side pieces, taking care to sew only up to the edge of the quilt top.

Finishing The Corners

You have three choices here – you can square the ends (Fig. A.), mitre the corners (Fig. D.) or insert a decorative corner (Fig. E.). Should you wish to mitre or insert, you will need additional fabric.

To mitre: place one border over the other. Use a pencil and ruler to draw a line between the quilt corner and the overlap corner (Fig. B.). Swap the uppermost border and draw the same line (Fig. C.).

Using the marked lines as sewing lines, carefully pin and sew from the innermost to the outer corner, Trim away the seam allowance leaving ¼" then press carefully.

For an inset corner: make a square block, either pieced or plain the size of your border width i.e. if your border is 4" finished width make a small block, pieced or plain, 4½" wide and sew it into place.

Quilting – Marking Your Design

Now your quilt top is complete. you will need to mark your quilting lines. If you plan to simply echo the lines on your blocks, then you will not need to mark, but any extra quilting needs to be carefully thought out. Quilting designs can come from many sources – often a project will have suggested designs, or there are books available both of designs and ideas of how to create your own. Choose your marking tool with care, some pencils etc may not easily wash or brush out. Experiment with as many as you can find on a separate fabric until you are satisfied. A light source in the shape of a light box or window will make marking the quilt top very much easier, especially on darker fabrics. Any straight lines should be drawn against a long ruler.

Sandwiching The Layers

Once you are satisfied that your design is clearly marked, and the backing fabric is

FIG. F.

FIG. G.

pressed, make a quilt 'sandwich' as follows: Lay your backing fabric on a flat surface, and make sure it is nice and smooth. Now place

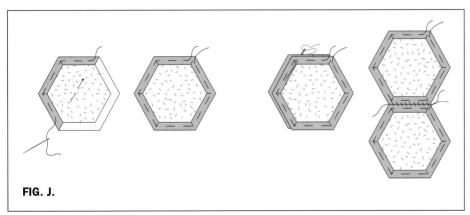

FIG. J.

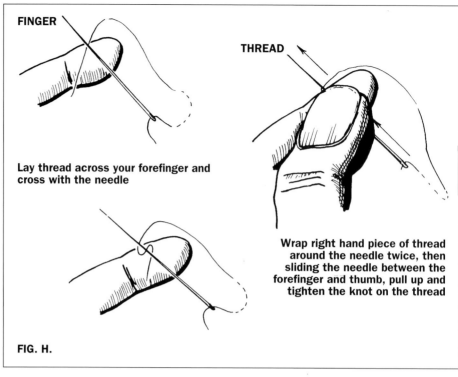

FINGER

Lay thread across your forefinger and cross with the needle

THREAD

Wrap right hand piece of thread around the needle twice, then sliding the needle between the forefinger and thumb, pull up and tighten the knot on the thread

FIG. H.

your wadding (Cut approx. 3" larger all round than the quilt top) on top of the backing and smooth that into place. Finally add the quilt top, taking care all the while that it is smooth. There are two ways to hold the three layers together for quilting. Either tack in both directions across the quilt, leaving approx. 4" between tacking lines, see Fig. F or pin evenly across the surface using fine safety pins, see Fig. G. These can be easily removed as your quilting progresses, but the tacking remains until the quilting is finished.

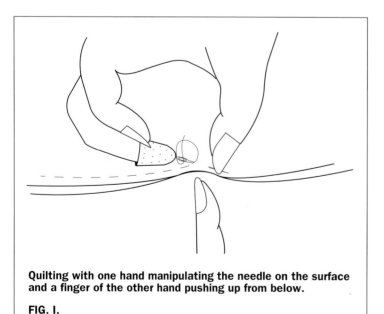

Quilting with one hand manipulating the needle on the surface and a finger of the other hand pushing up from below.

FIG. I.

Quilting– The Stitching Technique

The quilting stitch is basically a small neat running stitch, The idea is to hold the three layers of the quilt together in a way that is interesting and decorative in its own right. Quilting is best done with a 'between' needle, which is short and strong. Generally it is believed that the smaller the needle, the smaller the stitch, but you should start with the most comfortable size for you then graduate to a smaller needle. The higher the number i.e. 10 or 12, the smaller the needle. It is important to become used to using a thimble on the middle finger of the sewing hand because you will not be able to quilt for long without the finger getting very, very sore! Although the thimble will feel strange at first, it is worth persevering – before long you won't want to sew anything without it!

There are several ways to anchor your quilt at the correct tension for quilting; hoops and hand frames being the easiest and most convenient if you want to move around or pack it away every night. Always remember to remove your quilting from the hoop/frame if you are not going to quilt for a couple of hours. It can leave permanent creased marks otherwise. If you decide to invest in a floor frame you tack the quilt into place and leave it in until all the quilting is done. Try to have a go on a floor frame before committing yourself as they can be a hefty investment.

In general you should begin quilting in the middle of your piece and work towards the outside edges. If however it is thoroughly pinned or tacked, it will not make too much difference.

Quilting thread is readily available in a selection of colours and is the easiest to quilt with because it is fairly smooth and strong and less inclined to knot. Ordinary sewing cotton can be used, but running it through a cake of beeswax will make it stronger and smoother.

Thread your needle with a length of thread, approx. 17"-18", and do a quilters knot in the end, see Fig. H. Insert the needle into the quilt top, but only under the top, about ½" away from where the first stitch will begin, and bring the needle up and out again exactly where you want to start. Pulling the thread with a jerk will cause the knot to 'pop' through the fabric where it will stay among the wadding. Now take a small backstitch, coming out again just where the second stitch needs to start, and taking small neat stitches, start to quilt. Place your non sewing hand underneath the work so you can feel the needle when it comes through, and press with this hand to create a film tension from underneath. You will find this 'under' finger will need some protection too. Aim to place three or four even stitches on your needle at once, so you can develop the rocking motion which makes quilting even and also helps you to relax and enjoy it. Fig. I.

When you have finished a line of quilting or the thread is running out, tie a knot in the thread about ¼" from the surface of the quilt, and taking another backstitch lose this knot in the wadding.

When you are satisfied that all the quilting is complete, remove the tacking threads or the remaining pins and you are ready to finish off your quilt.

Machine Quilting

This is becoming much more popular nowadays and there are lots of books and equipment around to help you; they are well worth the investment Always practice on small pieces and graduate to larger ones, but do your home work first! Machine quilting can be quick and very effective, but can also be disastrous if it goes wrong.

Binding

Once all your quilting is completed, whether by hand or machine, you are ready to bind your project. First trim away the excess wadding and backing, so the edges are nice and even. There are several ways to finish the edges of a quilt; binding being very popular. You can use purchased bias binding, bias cut yourself from one of the fabrics in your quilt (the bias is essential if your corners are curved). For a quilt with straight sides, a double folded binding is easy and effective, as well as being durable. For this, cut a strip approximately 3" wide and the length of your quilt from one of your fabrics. Fold it in half lengthways with the edges meeting and pin these raw edges along the raw edges of the front of your quilt. Sew it into place taking ¼" seam allowance, then turn the folded edge to the back of your quilt and hem it down the entire length. Repeat with the opposite side, then the top and bottom edges, taking care to neatly over sew the edges at the corners.

To Finish

Now all that remains is to clearly mark your quilt with your name and the date and any other details you wish. This can be done with indelible marker onto a piece of fabric which you can hem into place on the back of the quilt; or you could cross-stitch a nice little label. Don't forget, this quilt could be an heirloom of the future!

suppliers

A Pocketful of Charms
Ingsdon
1 Highfield Close
Malvern Link
Worcs
WR14 1SH
Tel/Fax: 01684 893952
Batiste, charms, shadow trapunto kits, and much more. Send SAE for catalogue

P&Q
Oak Tree Cottage
Evesbatch
Bishops Frome
Worcs
WR6 5BE
Tel/Fax: 01531 640001
Large range of stencils and paints, send SAE for catalogue

Quilt Basics
Unit 19
Chiltern House
Waterside
Chesham
Bucks
HP5 1PS
Tel: 01494 791401
Large range of tools, quilting stencils, quilting equipment etc. Send 3 x 1st class stamps for mail order catalogue

R & R Enterprises
13 Frederick Road
Malvern
Worcs
WR14 1RS
Tel: 01684 563235
Universal craft frames in lightweight tubular PVC. Floor or hand frames. SAE for details

Strawberry Fayre
Chagford
Devon
TQ13 8EN
Tel: 01647 433250
Superb range of fabrics – Mail order only – send 8 x 1st class stamps for samples

Traplet Publications Ltd.
Traplet House
Severn Drive
Upton Upon Severn
Worcestershire
WR8 0JL
Tel: +44 (0) 1684 594505
Fax: +44 (0) 1684 594586
Email: traplet@dial.pipex.com

Patchwork & Quilting
The First & Best Loved Magazine For The True Enthusiast!
This bi-monthly magazine captures the fascination that quilting has held for millions of people over 100's of years. Projects, show reports, new products, competitions and a multitude of hints and tips.

£2.75 Bi-Monthly
Available The Third Friday Of Every Other Month!

Sewing World
The Only Magazine Of Its Kind!
Dedicated to machine stitchers the world over, Sewing World has experienced an explosion in popularity since its launch in Spring '95. From making outfits, to furnishings, to the care of fabrics, how to get the most from your sewing machine, Sewing World has it all.

£2.50 Monthly
Available The Third Friday Of Every Month!

Both of these magazines are available from your local newsagents, craft shop or direct from Traplet Publications Ltd